# St George for England

# St George for England

## SONGS & PLAYS
## FOR ST GEORGE'S DAY

*edited by*
*John Thor Ewing*

WELKIN BOOKS

First Published 2019
Welkin Books Ltd

Copyright © John Thor Ewing 2019

John Thor Ewing asserts his right to be identified as author of this edition, including notes, introduction and edited text, in accordance with the Design, Copyrights and Patents Act 1988

All rights reserved. No part of this publication may be reproduced, stored in a retrieval system, or transmitted in any form or by any means, without the prior written permission of the publisher, nor be otherwise circulated in any from of binding or cover other than that in which it is published and without a similar condition being imposed upon the subsequent purchaser.

ISBN 978-1-910075-10-4

# Acknowledgements

It has been a delight to re-explore the traditions of St George for this book. Some were very familiar to me, some less so, while others were dimly recalled from childhood reading. I am indebted as ever to my wife and family, and also to everyone who has performed with me in mumming plays.

I hope that discovering these songs, rhymes and plays will give others as much pleasure as it has given me, and that some of these old traditions of days gone by will be taken up again for St George's Day festivities in years to come.

JTE

# Contents

| | |
|---|---|
| *Introduction* | 8 |
|    *Songs of St George* | 11 |
|    *Plays of St George* | 13 |

### SONGS OF ST GEORGE

| | |
|---|---|
| *St George for England* | 20 |
| *The Birth of St George* | 24 |
| *St George and the Dragon* | 34 |
| *Great St George* | 48 |

### PLAYS OF ST GEORGE

| | |
|---|---|
| *St George and the Dragon* | 52 |
| *St George and Bold Slasher* | 62 |

### MUSIC FOR THE PLAYS

| | |
|---|---|
| *A-mumming we will go* | 70 |
| *Now our play is ended* | 70 |
| *Once I was dead* | 71 |

# Introduction

England has long celebrated the legend of St George. As early as the year 1222, St George was already so popular in England that St George's Day was declared a holiday by the Synod of Oxford. In the reign of King Edward III, St George was recognised as England's patron saint and the prime focus for national pride. And in 1415, the Archbishop of Canterbury declared that the feast of St George should be held in the same honour as Christmas Day.

St George's Day, 23rd April, is also celebrated as the birthday of William Shakespeare the national bard. Other anniversaries which fall on this date include the accession of Alfred the Great as King of Wessex in 871, and the coronation of King Charles II marking the Restoration of the Monarchy in 1661.

We know so little of the real historical St George that some scholars have doubted his existence, and it is of course impossible to find a historian who will vouch for the central episode of his life—his fight with the dragon. But what needs historical veracity? As with all great heroes, it is the legend of St George that is worth the telling, and it would be folly to submit the legend to the pedantic constraints of history, which has a disturbing habit of revealing our heroes to be just as flawed as ourselves.

There are still those who say that England should abandon St George for another saint, usually asserting that George is not genuinely English. But while it may be true that George was not originally from

England, he has become English through long association. Indeed, according to the legends in this book, St George was actually born in England, from where he was mysteriously spirited away to Cappadocia or Syria Palæstina, and it's still possible to visit the (admittedly slightly underwhelming) ruins of Caludon Castle in Coventry, where St George is supposed to have been born.

Unsurprisingly, English portrayals of St George were adapted to whatever cause the English supported. It was in 1098, when St George appeared to knights of the First Crusade at the Battle of Antioch that he became the ultimate crusader hero. This has led many to assume St George was an enemy of Islam, but his story is set long before the days of the Prophet Muhammad and, as well as Christian legends, there are also Muslim tales of St George (known in Arabic as Jiriyas or Girgus) which tell how the saint is able to bring the dead back to life—a theme which may be echoed in the play of 'St George and the Dragon.' Likewise for Protestant Englishmen, George could become a Protestant saint co-opted to support their opposition to Papal authority, while his appeal remained just as strong for English Catholics.

In English legend, St George is firmly linked with Egypt. It is there, according to English stories, that he defeats the dragon, and there he meets his beloved Sabra the King of Egypt's daughter. Although the first written evidence for this version of events dates only from Elizabethan times, it may have deeper roots in popular storytelling. For many centuries, English patriotism focussed on rivalry with France, and perhaps England's St George became associated with the King of Egypt after the disastrous French-led Seventh Crusade.

In 1229, al-Kamil the Ayyubid sultan of Egypt (known in the West as Meledin) had made peace with the crusaders and returned most of Jerusalem to Christian rule. Although a Muslim alliance of Mamluks and Khwarezmians took Jerusalem back in 1244, there was no enthusiasm for another crusade. Only the ultra-pious King Louis IX of France was determined to demonstrate his devotion to God by launching a crusade, not against Jerusalem but against Egypt. King Louis's crusade was almost entirely French, but he was joined by a small body of English knights, who were wiped out at the Battle of Al Mansourah along with their captain Sir William Longespée, the cousin of the English King Henry III. A few days after Longespée was killed, the French king himself was taken prisoner in Egypt and, ten weeks later, the Mamluks murdered the last Ayyubid sultan and seized control of Egypt for themselves. Sir William Longespée's heroic death was long remembered by the medieval English, who blamed his downfall not on the Ayyubid sultans of Egypt or even their Mamluk army, but on French arrogance, jealousy and cowardice.

It's tempting to hear echoes of these events in later retellings of the St George legend (and the medieval romance of Sir Bevis of Hampton which it closely resembles) where an alternative version of the tragic story of William Longespée is recast 'as it should have happened' so that our hero wins the good sultan's daughter as his bride, and the Mamluk threat (embodied in the figure of Bold Slasher, the Prince of Paradise or the Morocco King) is defeated.

But whatever historical events may have left their mark on the stories of St George, it is the stories themselves and, above all, the glorious swagger they embody, which are the essence of England's relationship with its national saint. England has shaped these legends, and has made St George into a very perfect English saint.

# Songs of St George

## *St George for England*

This song appears in several seventeenth-century broadsides (the earliest dated 1612) and it is mentioned both in Ben Jonson's play *Bartholomew Fair* and in Henry Fielding's novel *Tom Jones*. The text here is based on Percy's *Reliques of Ancient English Poetry*, but has been trimmed down from its original twelve verses. The last line of the chorus, 'Honi soit qui mal y pense,' is the motto of the Order of the Garter, England's highest order of chivalry, established by King Edward III in 1344 under the patronage of St George; it translates as 'Shame on him who thinks ill of it.'

I was able to find two versions of the music (Chappell, *Popular Music of the Olden Time*, p286-7, and B409 on the ABC Notation website) but neither is completely satisfactory, indeed both may be transcriptions of half-remembered tunes. Both these sources have contributed to the tune presented here, but I have reworked the melody to give more shape to the music of the verse. The tune is a slightly tricky one to memorise because it does not resolve until the first mention of St George in the last line of each verse, so that both words and music combine to emphasise the pre-eminence of St George among all heroes. This is an old-fashioned chorus song, where an experienced singer takes the verses and everyone joins in with the repeated refrain. I have included an optional harmony for the last line of each chorus, where the main tune follows the lower notes.

## The Birth of St George

The text is presented here more-or-less as it appears in Percy's *Reliques*, which I have set to one of the many traditional tunes used for the carol 'While Shepherds watched their Flocks.'

## St George and the Dragon

In his *Reliques of Ancient English Poetry*, Bishop Percy drew the text for this song from 'two ancient black-letter copies in the Pepys Collection' and I have followed his edition here. The melody is named on one of the surviving early broadsides as 'Flying Fame' but this tune will not fit the words, and it is set here to the tune 'Queen Dido, or Troy Town' with which 'Flying Fame' was sometimes confused. As with 'St George for England,' I have combined versions of the melody from Chappell and ABC Notation, but in this case the differences between the two were minimal.

## Great St George

The words of this hymn were composed by J. W. Reeks (1849-1900). The full text runs to six verses, of which I have chosen three. Three verses are also used in the Roman Catholic Divine Office for St George's Day, where the recommended hymn tune is 'Swavesey' composed by John Crookall (1821-87).

# Plays of St George

Several references to plays of St George from the fifteenth and sixteenth centuries have been collated by Prof. Clifford Davidson ('British Saint Play Records', 2002). Among the earliest is from 1431, when it was recorded that 'in this yeare was St Georges playes playd in Chester.' When King Edward IV entered Bristol in 1461, a pageant showed St George 'on horsbakke,' with a king and queen 'on hyghe in a castell,' and their daughter with a lamb, a dragon, and angels who provided 'greet melody' when the dragon was slain; a similar pageant was performed in Coventry in 1474 for the king's son, Edward, Prince of Wales, which included, as well as St George and the dragon, 'a kynges doughter knelyng afore hym with a lambe, and the fader & the moder beyng in a toure aboven beholdyng Seint George savyng their doughter from the dragon'. In Norwich in 1471, St George was to 'make a conflicte with the dragon and kepe his astate', while in Lydd the 'play of Seint George' was performed in 1489, and a new 'pley boke' was produced in 1531. There are records of other early performances at Ipswich, Leicester, Thame, Hereford, York, Bassingbourn, Morebath, Lostwithiel, London and Wells, as well as more surprisingly at Dublin and Aberdeen.

The king and queen in their castle tower and the princess with her lamb, which featured in fifteenth-century performances at Bristol and Coventry, also appear in contemporary illustrations from *Constitutiones legitime sue legatine regionis anglicane*, 1504 (reproduced here on p6) and from Alexander Barclay's *Life of St George*, 1511 (p18). Surviving speeches from these early plays emphasise St George's role as guardian of England.

Both the plays in this book are composite texts, for which I have drawn on a range of sources, most of which are available at the website www.folkplay.info. These traditional 'mumming' plays are clearly not identical with the plays performed for medieval English kings, but there is no reason to doubt they have roots in those older performances. Whilst almost every individual line of the two plays is drawn from tradition, neither play is primarily derived from any single exemplar, and the choice and arrangement of lines is such that each version constitutes a unique original work in its own right.

Some readers may be disappointed that between both plays there is just one female role and, even when she does appear, Fair Sabra hardly gets a look in, with a mere three lines of 'dialogue'. Throughout the eighteenth and nineteenth centuries, the mummers who performed these plays were working men in traditional communities, and a romantic female role which offered little opportunity for humour was unlikely to have been popular with such actors. Although Sabra's role appears in printed texts, it is omitted entirely from most traditional versions of the play. Sabra does play a greater role in the legend of St George, and there is of course no reason why modern performers shouldn't expand on Sabra's part in the play, should they so wish. The role of St George can also work well when played by a young woman in the pantomime tradition of the principal boy.

A similar logic explains why the dragon is usually omitted, as he is in the play of 'St George and Bold Slasher' here. Although he might seem essential to the story of St George, it is clear from the so-called 'Oxfordshire Christmas Miracle Play' (published in *Notes and Queries*, Series 5, Vol. II, pp.503-5) where the dragon performs somersaults in his battle with St George, that the dragon's part could be the most physically demanding role in the play. Whereas other parts can be performed in a more-or-less desultory manner, the dragon must use some form of physical theatre to communicate its non-human nature.

The English mumming tradition is frequently associated with Christmas, and both these plays would be equally at home as Christmas mumming plays, when the character of Prologue or Sir Guy would be replaced by Old Father Christmas with the additional lines,

Welcome here, or welcome not,

I hope Father Christmas shall never be forgot.

In performance, a mummers' play should be 'acted out' rather than acted. The words are to be declaimed, with attention paid to clarity, rhythm and rhyme, more than to feeling or character. This is a dramatic performance akin to pantomime and street theatre, and is very far from any attempt at realism. Performances may be wooden, may be hammy, may be bombastic, but there is little room for subtlety.

## St George and the Dragon

This text explores what I take to be the original story underlying the tradition of St George plays, which is broadly similar to the plot of the ballad of 'St George and the Dragon.' It draws on some of the earliest recorded oral versions of the play as well as early printed editions. Most of the oral versions I looked at were from the eighteenth century (a particularly interesting source was the Truro play published in *Notes and Queries*, Series 12, Vol. I, pp.390-3, which has recently been re-dated to the late 1780's) but, because there are relatively few examples of plays which include the role of the Dragon, I stretched the net somewhat wider for Dragon plays.

I have corrected what seem to me to be errors, even where they are generally accepted in all the traditional plays. Most importantly, in traditional versions of this play the King of Egypt makes separate claims that both George and the Prince of Paradise (aka Bold Slasher) are his only son, and in some plays (as in the play of 'St George and

Bold Slasher' here) these two opponents are explicitly described as brothers. This makes no sense. Apart from the fact that they cannot both be the only son of the same man, St George is adamant that he is English and that he will marry the King of Egypt's daughter—as he himself explains in the play, he wins his position in Egypt through killing the Dragon.

It seems the Prince of Paradise must be the King of Egypt's true son, and the confusion has come about because the King of Egypt explains his backstory immediately before introducing the character of St George, so that at some point, the King of Egypt's lines about his son have been mistakenly applied to St George. I have assumed that the play incorporates a widespread folktale motif whereby the King of Egypt offers his kingdom and his daughter's hand in marriage to whoever will slay the Dragon. After St George unexpectedly succeeds in this task, the King of Egypt's real son attempts to overturn this offer by challenging St George to combat. To clear up the confusion with minimal alteration to the traditional words, I have rewritten the King of Egypt's speech to include lines adapted from St George's speech after the dragon fight, so that when they are spoken again by St George it is in fulfilment of the terms set out earlier by the King of Egypt.

I have also accepted the suggestion of E K Chambers (*The English Folk Play*, 1933, p178) that the words usually attributed to Bold Slasher ('My head is made of iron, my body made of steel, &c.') rightly belong to the dragon.

Following the hint in Muslim legends which make St George a healer as much as a warrior, with the power to restore the dead to life, it would seem possible that the character of the Doctor was originally an extension of the role of St George. The play may be easily adapted so that this is the case, but I expect most mummers will prefer to keep the distinction between the two parts.

The song, 'A-mumming we will go' is adapted from the version in Juliana Horatia Ewing's play 'The Peace Egg.' Mrs Ewing, who grew up as Julie Gatty near Sheffield in the mid-nineteenth century, wrote that, although the song did not feature in printed texts, 'I never saw mumming without it.'

## St George and Bold Slasher

The second play was originally put together for performance as part of a Christmas evening's entertainment, and has gone through several incarnations since. In contrast with 'St George and the Dragon,' it aims to be short and sweet, with an emphasis purely on light-hearted fun. The sources for this play are traditional plays from the North East of England and the Scottish Borders.

# SONGS OF ST GEORGE

# St George for England

adapted by J T Ewing

# St George for England

1.
Why do you boast of Arthur and his knights,
Knowing well how many men have endurëd fights?
For besides King Arthur and Lancelot du Lake
Or Sir Tristram de Lionel that fought for ladies sake,
Read in old histories, and there you shall see
How St George, St George the dragon made to flee.

*St George he was for England, St Dennis was for France;*
*Sing, 'Honi soit qui mal y pense.'*

2.
The wars of ancient monarchs it were too long to tell,
And likewise of the Romans, how far they did excel—
Hannibal and Scipio in many a field did fight,
Orlando Furioso he was a worthy knight,
Remus and Romulus were they that Rome did build,
But St George, St George the dragon made to yield.

*St George he was for England, St Dennis was for France;*
*Sing, 'Honi soit qui mal y pense.'*

3.
Richard Cœur de Lion, erst king of this land,
He the lion gorëd with his naked hand;
The false Duke of Austria nothing did he fear,
But his son he killed with a box upon the ear,
Besides his famous acts done in the Holy Land,
But St George, St George the dragon did withstand.

*St George he was for England, St Dennis was for France;*
*Sing, 'Honi soit qui mal y pense.'*

4.       Henry the Fifth he conquerëd all France,
And quartered their arms, his honour to advance,
He their cities razëd and threw their castles down,
And his head he honoured with a double crown;
He thumped the Frenchmen and after home he came,
But St George, St George he did the dragon tame.

*St George he was for England, St Dennis was for France;*
*Sing, 'Honi soit qui mal y pense.'*

5.       St David of Wales the Welshmen much advance,
St Jaques of Spain, that never yet broke lance,
St Patrick of Ireland, which was St George's boy,
Seven years he kept his horse and then stole him away,
And the Scots unto death will St Andrew maintain,
But St George, St George the dragon he hath slain.

*St George he was for England, St Dennis was for France;*
*Sing, 'Honi soit qui mal y pense.'*

# The Birth of St George

Traditional

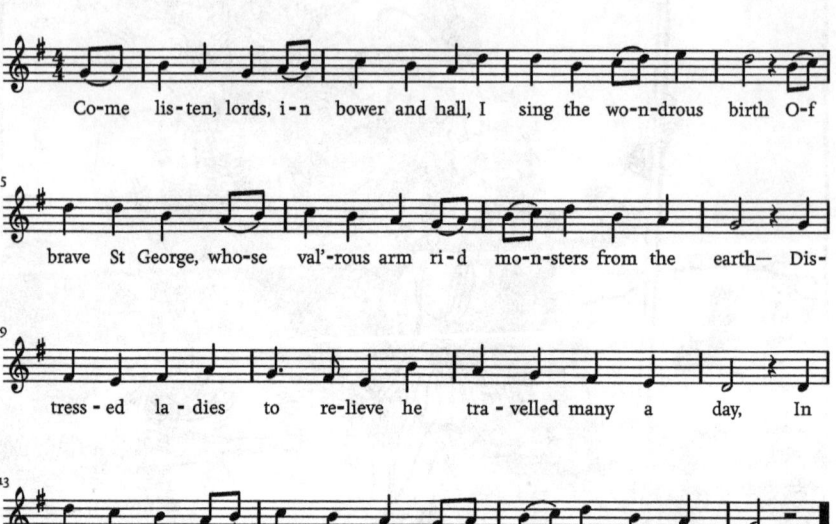

Come listen, lords, in bower and hall, I sing the wondrous birth Of brave St George, whose val'rous arm rid monsters from the earth— Distressed ladies to relieve he travelled many a day, In honour of the holy faith, which shall endure for aye.

# The Birth of St George

1.
    Come listen, lords, in bower and hall,
        I sing the wondrous birth
   Of brave St George, whose valorous arm
      Rid monsters from the earth—
      Distressëd ladies to relieve
       He travelled many a day,
     In honour of the holy faith,
      Which shall endure for aye.

2.
     In Coventry sometime did dwell
       A knight of worthy fame,
   High steward of this noble realm,
      Lord Albert was his name.
    He had to wife, a princely dame,
       Whose beauty did excel—
  This virtuous lady, being with child,
      In sudden sadness fell.

3.
    For thirty nights, no sooner sleep
      Had closed her wakeful eyes,
   But lo! a foul and fearful dream
      Her fancy would surprise—
   She dreamt a dragon fierce and fell
     Conceived within her womb,
  Whose mortal fangs her body rent,
     Ere he to life could come.

4.      All woe-begone and sad was she;
She nourished constant woe,
Yet strove to hide it from her lord,
Lest he should sorrow know—
In vain she strove, her tender lord
Who watched her slightest look,
Discovered soon her secret pain,
And in that pain partook.

5.      And when to him the fearful cause
She weeping did impart,
With kindest speech he strove to heal
The anguish of her heart:
"Be comforted, my lady dear,
Those pearly drops refrain;
Betide me weal, betide me woe,
I'll try to ease thy pain.

6.      "And for this foul and fearful dream,
That causeth all thy woe,
Trust me, I'll travel far away,
But I'll the meaning know."
Then giving many a fond embrace,
And shedding many a tear,
To the weïrd lady of the woods
He purposed to repair.

7.    To the weïrd lady of the woods,
Full long and many a day,
Through lonely shades and thickets rough,
He wends his weary way.
At length he reached a dreary dell
With dismal yews o'erhung,
Where cypress spread its mournful boughs
And poisonous nightshade sprung.

8.    No cheerful gleams here pierced the gloom,
He hears no cheerful sound,
But shrill night-ravens' yelling scream
And serpents hissing round;
The shriek of fiends and damned ghosts
Ran howling through his ear—
A chilling horror froze his heart,
Though all unused to fear.

9.    Three times he strives to win his way
And pierce those sickly dews,
Three times to bear his trembling corse
His knocking knees refuse;
At length, upon his beating breast
He signs the holy cross,
And rousing up his wonted might,
He treads the unhallowed moss.

10.        Beneath a pendant craggy cliff,
All vaulted like a grave,
An opening in the solid rock
He found the enchanted cave—
An iron gate closed up the mouth,
All hideous and forlorn,
Where fastened by a silver chain,
There hung a brazëd horn.

11.        Then offering up a secret prayer,
Three times he blows amain;
Three times a deep and hollow sound
Did answer him again.
"Sir knight, thy lady bears a son
Who, like a dragon bright,
Shall prove most dreadful to his foes,
And terrible in fight.

12.        "His name advanced in future times
On banners shall be worn,
But lo! thy lady's life must pass
Before he can be born."
All sore oppressed with fear and doubt,
Long time Lord Albert stood—
At length, he winds his doubtful way
Back through the dreary wood.

13.  Eager to clasp his lovely dame
    Then fast he travels back,
    But when he reached his castle gate,
    The gate was hung with black.
    In every court and hall he found
    A sullen silence reign,
    Save where, amid the lonely towers,
    He heard her maidens' plain.

14.  They bitterly lament and weep
    With many a grievous groan,
    So sore his bleeding heart misgave
    His lady's life was gone.
    With faltering step he enters in,
    Yet half afraid to go—
    With trembling voice asks why they grieve,
    Yet fears the cause to know.

15.  "Three times the sun hath rose and set,"
    They said then stopped to weep,
    "Since heaven hath laid thy lady dear
    In death's eternal sleep,
    For ah! in travail sore she fell,
    So sore that she must die,
    Unless some shrewd and cunning leech
    Could ease her presently.

16.    "But when a cunning leech was fetched,
Full soon declared he,
She or her babe must lose its life—
Both saved could not be.
'Now take my life,' thy lady said,
'My little infant save,
And O, commend me to my lord,
When I am laid in grave.

17.    "'O, tell him how that precious babe
Cost him a tender wife
And teach my son to lisp her name,
Who died to save his life.'
Then calling still upon thy name,
And praying still for thee,
Without repining or complaint,
Her gentle soul did flee."

18.    What tongue can paint Lord Albert's woe,
The bitter tears he shed,
The bitter pangs that wrung his heart
To find his lady dead?
He beat his breast, he tore his hair,
And shedding many a tear,
At last he asked to see his son,
The son that cost so dear.

19.  New sorrow seized the damsels all—
At length, they faltering say,
"Alas! My lord, how shall we tell?
Thy son is stolen away.
Fair as the sweetest flower of spring,
Such was his infant mien,
And on his little body stamped
Three wondrous marks were seen:

20.  "A blood-red cross was on his arm,
A dragon on his breast,
A little garter all of gold
Was round his leg expressed.
Three nurses then did we provide
Our little lord to keep—
One gave him suck, one gave him food,
And one did lull to sleep.

21.  "But lo! all in the dead of night,
We heard a fearful sound—
Loud thunder clapped, the castle shook
And lightning flashed around.
Dead with affright at first we lay,
But rousing up anon,
We ran to see our little lord—
Our little lord was gone!

22.     "But how or where we could not tell
            For, lying on the ground,
        In deep and magic slumbers laid,
            The nurses there we found."
        "O grief on grief!" Lord Albert said—
            No more his tongue could say,
        For falling in a deadly swoon,
            Long time he lifeless lay.

23.     And when restored to life and sense,
            He nourished endless woe—
        No future joy his heart could taste,
            No future comfort know.
        So withers on the mountain top
            A fair and stately oak,
        Whose vigorous arms are torn away
            By some rude thunder-stroke.

24.     In time his castle irksome grows,
            He loathes his wonted home;
        His native country he forsakes
            In foreign lands to roam.
        There up and down he wandered far,
            Clad in a pilgrim's gown;
        Till his brown locks grew white as wool,
            His beard as thistle down.

25.     At length, all wearied, down in death
        He laid his reverend head.
    Meantime, amid the lonely wilds
        His little son was bred.
    The weïrd lady of the woods
        Had borne him far away,
    And trained him up in feats of arms,
        And every martial play.

# St George and the Dragon

Traditional

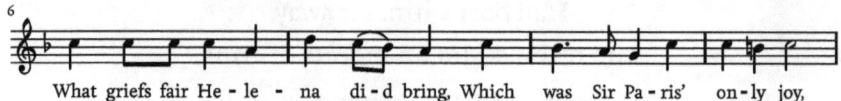

# St George and the Dragon

1.
    Of Hector's deeds did Homer sing,
    And of the sack of stately Troy,
    What griefs fair Helena did bring,
    Which was Sir Paris' only joy,
    And by my pen I will recite
    St George's deeds, an English knight.

2.
    Against the Saracens so rude
    Fought he full long and many a day,
    Where many giants he subdued,
    In honour of the Christian way,
    And after many adventures past
    To Egypt's land he came at last.

3.
    Now, as the story plain doth tell,
    Within that country there did rest
    A dreadful dragon fierce and fell,
    Whereby they were full sore oppressed,
    Who by his poisonous breath each day,
    Did many of the city slay.

4.
    The grief whereof did grow so great
    Throughout the limits of the land,
    That they their wise men did entreat
    To show their cunning out of hand—
    What way they might this fiend destroy,
    That did the country thus annoy.

5.         The wise men all before the king
             This answer framed incontinent:
           The dragon none to death might bring
             By any means they could invent;
         His skin more hard than brass was found,
        That sword nor spear could pierce nor wound.

6.         When this the people understood,
             They cried out most piteously,
           The dragon's breath infects their blood,
             That every day in heaps they die;
            Among them such a plague it bred,
           The living scarce could bury the dead.

7.         No means there were, as they could hear,
             For to appease the dragon's rage,
             But to present some virgin clear,
           Whose blood his fury might assuage;
             Each day he would a maiden eat,
              For to allay his hunger great.

8.         This thing by art the wise men found,
             Which truly must observed be,
           Wherefore throughout the city round
             A virgin pure of good degree
            Was by the king's commission still
            Taken up to serve the dragon's will.

9.  Thus did the dragon every day
    Untimely crop some virgin flower,
    Till all the maids were worn away,
    And none were left him to devour,
    Saving the king's fair daughter bright,
    Her father's only heart's delight.

10. Then came the officers to the king
    That heavy message to declare,
    Which did his heart with sorrow sting—
    "She is," quoth he, "my kingdom's heir.
    O let us all be poisoned here,
    Ere she should die, that is my dear."

11. Then rose the people presently,
    And to the king in rage they went;
    They said his daughter dear should die,
    The dragon's fury to prevent.
    "Our daughters all are dead," quoth they,
    "And have been made the dragon's prey.

12. "And by their blood we rescued were,
    And thou hast saved thy life thereby;
    And now in sooth it is but fair,
    For us thy daughter so should die."
    "O save my daughter," said the king,
    "And let ME feel the dragon's sting."

13.    Then fell Fair Sabra on her knee,
And to her father dear did say,
"O Father, strive not thus for me,
But let me be the dragon's prey—
It may be, for my sake alone
This plague upon the land was thrown.

14.    "'Tis better I should die," she said,
"Than all your subjects perish quite;
Perhaps the dragon here was laid,
For my offence to work his spite,
And after he hath sucked my gore,
Your land shall feel the grief no more."

15.    "What hast thou done, my daughter dear,
For to deserve this heavy scourge?
It is my fault, as may appear,
Which makes the gods our state to purge—
Then ought I die, to stint the strife,
And to preserve thy happy life."

16.    Like mad men, all the people cried,
"Thy death to us can do no good.
Our safety only doth abide
In making her the dragon's food."
"Lo! here I am, I come," quoth she,
"Therefore do what you will with me."

17.     "Nay stay, dear daughter," quoth the queen,
        "And as thou art a virgin bright,
        That hast for virtue famous been,
        So let me clothe thee all in white,
        And crown thy head with flowers sweet,
        An ornament for virgins meet."

18.     And when she was attired so,
        According to her mother's mind,
        Unto the stake then did she go,
        To which her tender limbs they bind,
        And being bound to stake a thrall,
        She bade farewell unto them all.

19.     "Farewell, my father dear," quoth she,
        "And my sweet mother meek and mild,
        Take you no thought nor weep for me,
        For you may have another child—
        Since for my country's good I die,
        Death I receive most willingly."

20.     The king and queen and all their train
        With weeping eyes went then their way,
        And let their daughter there remain,
        To be the hungry dragon's prey,
        But as she did there weeping lie,
        Behold St George came riding by.

21. And seeing there a lady bright
So rudely tied unto a stake,
As well became a valiant knight,
He straight to her his way did take.
"Tell me, sweet maiden," then quoth he,
"What caitiff thus abuseth thee?

22. "And lo! by Christ his cross I vow,
Which here is figured on my breast,
I will revenge it on his brow,
And break my lance upon his chest."
And speaking thus whereas he stood,
The dragon issued from the wood.

23. The lady that did first espy
The dreadful dragon coming so,
Unto St George aloud did cry,
And willed him away to go—
"Here comes that cursed fiend," quoth she;
"That soon will make an end of me."

24. St George then looking round about,
The fiery dragon soon espied,
And like a knight of courage stout,
Against him did most fiercely ride,
And with such blows he did him greet,
He fell beneath his horse's feet.

25.   For with his lance that was so strong,
          As he came gaping in his face,
          In at his mouth he thrust along,
          For he could pierce no other place,
          And thus within the lady's view
     This mighty dragon straight he slew.

26.   The savour of his poisoned breath
          Could do this holy knight no harm.
          Thus he the lady saved from death,
          And home he led her by the arm,
          Which when King Ptolemy did see,
     There was great mirth and melody.

27. Whenas that valiant champion there
Had slain the dragon in the field,
To court he brought the lady fair,
Which to their hearts much joy did yield.
He in the court of Egypt stayed
Till he most falsely was betrayed.

28. That lady dearly loved the knight,
He counted her his only joy;
But when their love was brought to light
It turned unto their great annoy:
The Morocco king was in the court,
Who to the orchard did resort.

29. Daily to take the pleasant air,
For pleasure's sake he used to walk,
Under a wall he oft did hear
St George with Lady Sabra talk—
Their love he showed unto the king,
Which to St George great woe did bring.

30. Those kings together did devise
To make the Christian knight away,
With letters him in courteous wise
They straightway sent to Persia,
But wrote to the Sophy him to kill,
And treacherously his blood to spill.

31.  Thus they for good did him reward
            With evil, and most subtly
        By much vile means they had regard
            To work his death most cruelly,
        Who, as through Persia land he rode,
        With zeal destroyed each idol god.

32.  For which offence he straight was thrown
            Into a dungeon dark and deep,
        Where, when he thought his wrongs upon,
            He bitterly did wail and weep,
        Yet like a knight of courage stout,
        At length his way he digged out.

33.  Three grooms of the King of Persia
            By night this valiant champion slew,
        Though he had fasted many a day,
            And then away from thence he flew
        On the best steed the Sophy had,
        Which when he knew, he was full mad.

34.  Towards Christendom he made his flight,
            But met a giant by the way,
        With whom in combat he did fight
            Most valiantly a summer's day,
        Who yet, for all his bats of steel,
        Was forced the sting of death to feel.

35.    Back o'er the seas with many bands
         Of warlike soldiers soon he past,
         Vowing upon those heathen lands
         To work revenge, which at the last,
      Ere thrice three years were gone and spent,
         He wrought unto his heart's content.

36.    Save only Egypt's land he spared
         For Sabra bright her only sake,
         And, ere for her he had regard,
         He meant a trial kind to make—
      Meanwhile the king, o'ercome in field,
         Unto St George did quickly yield.

37.    Then straight Morocco's king he slew,
         And took Fair Sabra to his wife,
         But meant to try if she were true
         Ere with her he would lead his life,
      And, though he had her in his train,
         She did a virgin pure remain.

38.    Toward England then that lovely dame
         The brave St George conducted strait,
         An eunuch also with them came,
         Who did upon the lady wait—
      These three from Egypt went alone.
         Now mark St George's valour shown.

39.
    Whenas they in a forest were,
    The lady did desire to rest;
    Meanwhile St George to kill a deer,
    For their repast did think it best,
    Leaving her with the eunuch there,
    Whilst he did go to kill the deer.

40.
    But lo! all in his absence came
    Two hungry lions fierce and fell,
    And tore the eunuch on the same
    In pieces small, the truth to tell;
    Down by the lady then they laid,
    Whereby they showed, she was a maid.

41.
    But when he came from hunting back,
    And did behold this heavy chance,
    Then for his lovely virgin's sake
    His courage strait he did advance,
    And came into the lions' sight,
    Who ran at him with all their might.

42.
    Their rage did him no whit dismay,
    Who, like a stout and valiant knight,
    Did both the hungry lions slay
    Within the Lady Sabra's sight:
    Who all this while, sad and demure,
    There stood most like a virgin pure.

43.   Now when St George did surely know
        This lady was a virgin true,
       His heart was glad, that erst was woe,
        And all his love did soon renew—
         He set her on a palfrey steed,
       And towards England came with speed.

44.   Where, being in short space arrived
        Unto his native dwelling place,
       Therein with his dear love he lived,
        And fortune did his nuptials grace—
         They many years of joy did see,
       And led their lives at Coventry.

# Great St George
## SWAVESEY

J. W. Reeks 1849-1900

John Crookall 1821-87

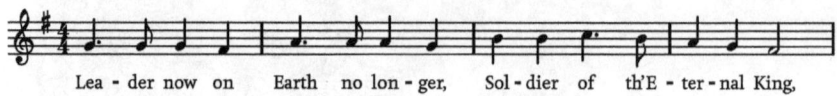
Lea-der now on Earth no lon-ger, Sol-dier of th'E-ter-nal King,

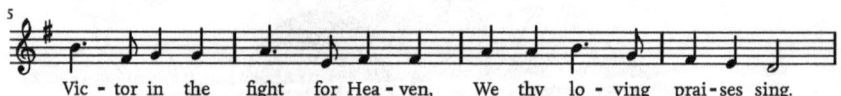
Vic-tor in the fight for Hea-ven, We thy lo-ving prai-ses sing.

Great St George, our pa-tron, help us, In the con-flict be thou nigh;

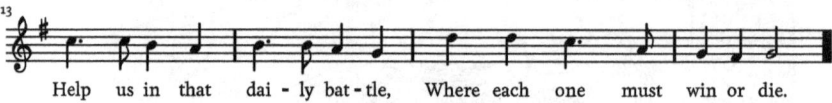
Help us in that dai-ly bat-tle, Where each one must win or die.

# Great St George

1.
Leader now on Earth no longer,
Soldier of the Eternal King,
Victor in the fight for Heaven,
We thy loving praises sing.

*Great St George, our patron, help us,*
*In the conflict be thou nigh;*
*Help us in that daily battle,*
*Where each one must win or die.*

2.
Clothe us in thy shining armour,
Place thy good sword in our hand;
Teach us how to wield it, fighting
Onward towards the heavenly land.

*Great St George, our patron, help us,*
*In the conflict be thou nigh;*
*Help us in that daily battle,*
*Where each one must win or die.*

3.
Onward, till, our striving over,
On life's battlefield we fall,
Resting then, but ever ready,
Waiting for the angel's call.

*Great St George, our patron, help us,*
*In the conflict be thou nigh;*
*Help us in that daily battle,*
*Where each one must win or die.*

J. W. Reeks, 1849—1900

# PLAYS OF ST GEORGE

# St George and the Dragon

DRAMATIS PERSONÆ:
   SIR GUY OF WARWICK
   KING OF EGYPT
   DRAGON
   FAIR SABRA
   PRINCE OF PARADISE
   DOCTOR

SIR GUY:
   Open your doors, and let us in,
   I hope your favour we shall win,
   For in this room there shall be shown
   The finest battle that ever was known,
   But whether we stand or whether we fall,
   We'll do our best to please you all.

[*All the mummers come in singing, and walk round the performance area in a circle, then stand to one side.*]

ALL [*sing*]:
   And a-mumming we will go, will go,
   And a-mumming we will go,
   And all for England and St George,
   A-mumming we will go!

[*Repeat ad lib until all actors are assembled.*]

SIR GUY:
>Room, room, brave gallants, room,
>Come give us room to rhyme,
>For in this house we mean to show
>Something of our past time.
>St George is at the door, and swears he will come in,
>With sword and shield at his side, I fear he'll pierce my skin.
>If you won't believe what I do say,
>Come in the King of Egypt, and clear the way!

KING OF EGYPT:
>Here I, the King of Egypt, so boldly do appear,
>The Prince of Paradise, he is my only son and heir,
>And fair Princess Sabra, my lovely daughter dear.
>St George, he is a worthy champion bold,
>That hopes to win our three crowns of gold:
>But he must fight the fiery dragon, and bring him to the slaughter;
>Before ever he can win my kingdom or my daughter.
>Walk in, walk in, St George, and boldly act your part,
>That all the people here may see your wondrous art.
>If you won't believe what I do say,
>Step in St George, and clear the way!

ST GEORGE:
>Here come I, St George, from England did I spring,
>I'll fight the Dragon bold, my wonders to begin.
>I'll clip his wings, he shall not fly:
>I'll cut him down, or else I die.

DRAGON:
   Who's he that seeks the Dragon's blood,
   And calls so angry and so loud?

ST GEORGE:
   I'm he who seeks the Dragon's blood
   And calls so angry and so loud.
   I am St George, that valiant knight,
   I'll spend my blood for England's right.

DRAGON:
   My head is made of iron, my body made of steel,
   My arms and legs of beaten brass; no man can make me feel.
   With my long teeth and scaly jaws,
   Of such as you I'd eat half a score
   And sate my stomach till I get more.

ST GEORGE:
   To battle, to battle, with you I will try
   To see who on this ground shall lie.

[*As they fight, the dragon chants.*]

DRAGON:
   Meat, meat, meat to eat!
   I am the dragon, here are my jaws,
   I am the dragon, here are my claws.
   Meat, meat, meat to eat!

[*St George slays the dragon, who leaves to rejoin the other actors. Fair Sabra steps forward.*]

FAIR SABRA:
   I am the Princess Sabra, and it is my delight,
   My chiefest pride, to be the bride
   Of this most gallant knight.

ST GEORGE:
   I am St George, that worthy champion bold,
   And with my glittering sword and spear I've won three crowns of gold:
   I've fought the fiery dragon, and brought him to the slaughter;
   And by that means I've won Fair Sabra, the King of Egypt's daughter.
   Seven long years in a close cave I was kept,
   And from there into a prison leapt;
   And from there onto a rock of stone,
   Where I made my sad and grievous moan.
   Many a giant did I subdue;
   I ran the fiery dragon through and through;
   I freed Fair Sabra from the stake;
   What more could mortal man undertake?
   I fought them all courageously,
   And still have gained the victory.
   Show me the man that dares bid me stand,
   I'll cut him down with my courageous hand.

KING OF EGYPT:
   Come in, come in my eldest son,
   And show how battles are lost or won.

PRINCE OF PARADISE:
   I am the Prince of Paradise, born of high renown;
   Soon will I fetch St George's lofty courage down.
   'Twas I that slew the Seven Brethren, but for them I did not care,
   For through their hearts I ran my glittering sword and spear.
   I'll fight St George, who is my foe,
   I'll make him yield before I go.

ST GEORGE:
   Stand off, Prince of Paradise, or by my sword you'll die.
   I'll pierce your body full of holes, and make your buttons fly.
   For England's right and admiration,
   Here I draw my bloody weapon;
   Pull out your sword and fight, or pull out your purse and pay—
   I'll have satisfaction before I go away.

PRINCE OF PARADISE:
   No satisfaction shall you have,
   But I will bring you to your grave.

ST GEORGE:
   To battle, to battle with you I call,
   To see who on this ground shall fall.

PRINCE OF PARADISE:
   To battle, to battle with you I pray,
   To see who on this ground shall lay.

[*They fight until the Prince of Paradise falls, dropping his sword.*]

O pardon me, St George, pardon I crave,
O pardon me this night, and I will be your slave.

ST GEORGE:
No pardon shall you have, while you can yet stand,
So get up again and fight, with your sword in your hand.

[*They fight again, and St George kills the Prince of Paradise.*]

Now ladies and gentlemen, see what I have done,
I have cut him down like the evening sun.
Take him away and give him to the flies,
For I will not behold him any longer with my eyes.

KING OF EGYPT:
O cruel Christian, what have you done?
You have wounded and killed my only son.

ST GEORGE:
Why should I not kill him, my honour to maintain,
For if he could, he would have done to me the same?

KING OF EGYPT:
O cruel Christian, why did you have to kill,
Or on the ground his precious blood to spill?

ST GEORGE:
He challenged me to fight and why should I deny?
See how low he lies who held himself so high!

KING OF EGYPT:
>   Step in Sir Guy of Warwick, and help me in my need,
>   For on the ground my son and heir does bleed.

SIR GUY:
>   Is there never a doctor to be found
>   Or to be had this night,
>   To heal our prince of his deep and deadly wound,
>   And make him stand up right?

DOCTOR:
>   O yes, there is a doctor to be found
>   All ready, near at hand,
>   To heal your prince of his deep and deadly wound,
>   And make the dead man stand.
>   I am a doctor, pure and good,
>   And with my sword, I'll staunch his blood.

SIR GUY:
>   O Doctor, Doctor, what can you cure?

DOCTOR:
>   I am the doctor to cure all ill:
>   I have plaster and potion, poison and pill,
>   Some will cure, and some will kill,
>   All sorts of diseases, just as I pleases,
>   The itch, the stitch, the palsy and the gout;
>   All aches within and pains without;
>   If the devil's within, I'll soon cast him out.

SIR GUY:
   O Doctor, Doctor, where have you travelled?

DOCTOR:
   I've travelled through England, France and Spain
   To cure the man that here lies slain.

SIR GUY:
   O Doctor, Doctor, what is your fee?

DOCTOR:
   Fifteen pound, it is my fee,
   The money to lay down,
   But as it's for His Majesty,
   I'll do it for ten pound.

SIR GUY:
   Take it—

DOCTOR:
   I have a little bottle by my side;
   The fame of it spreads far and wide.
   The stuff therein is elecampane;
   It will bring the dead to life again.
   Here, Jack, take some of my nip-nap
   And pour it down your tip-tap,
   A drop on his head, a drop on his heart.
   Rise up, bold prince, and take your part.
   Hocus pocus, elecampane,
   Rise up, and come to life again!

PRINCE OF PARADISE:
   What place is here? What scenes appear
   Wherever I turn my eyes?
   For all around is enchanted ground,
   And soft illusions rise.
   It is on hallowed ground we walk,
   By flowery mountains and mossy fountains,
   A hundred voices round us talk,
   From hill to hill, the voices tossed,
   On rocks rebounding, echoes sounding,
   And not a single word is lost.
   Aloft, aloft, where I have been,
   What strange and foreign lands I've seen!
   I have been half-puffed and huddled in the sky;
   These moons and stars caused me to die.

ST GEORGE:
   Oh, horrible! Oh, terrible! The like was never seen—
   A man driven out of seven senses, and into seventeen.

PRINCE OF PARADISE:
   O dear honoured father leave off your sad grief,
   For here you see I'm risen, and here you see I live.
   Now hark! St George, I hear the silver trumpet sound,
   That summons me from off this bloody ground.
   The trumpet sounds, I must away.
   Farewell, St George. I can no longer stay.

[*The Prince of Paradise leaves.*]

ST GEORGE:
> Farewell, Prince of Paradise. Bear news to your own land
> And tell what a bold champion there does in England stand.
> Old England's right I will maintain
> And I'll fight for England once again!

[*St George leaves.*]

SIR GUY:
> So, ladies and gentlemen, our sport is now ended
> I hope none of you have been offended.
> My hat is dumb and cannot speak—
> Pray put something in it for St George's sake;
> The hat it would speak, if it had but a tongue—
> Come throw in your money, and think it no wrong.

[*Sir Guy passes the hat around. The cast may sing 'Now our play is ended' from the play of 'St George and Bold Slasher' or, as an alternative to his final speech after St George has left the stage, Sir Guy may sing 'St George for England' with the rest of the cast joining in the chorus.*]

# St George and Bold Slasher

DRAMATIS PERSONÆ:
   PROLOGUE
   ST GEORGE
   BOLD SLASHER
   DR BROWN

PROLOGUE:
   Open the door!
   Up sticks and up stools,
   Here there comes a pack of fools.
   Stir up the fire and strike a light,
   For in this house there'll be a fight.
   If you don't believe these words I say,
   Step in St George and clear the way!

ST GEORGE:
   In comes I, St George; St George it is my name.
   With sword and spear by my side, I hope to win the game.

BOLD SLASHER:
   The game, sir?

ST GEORGE:
              The game, sir, is not within your power—
   I'll cut you into ribbons, in under half an hour.

BOLD SLASHER:
　You, sir?

ST GEORGE:
　　　　　I, sir!

BOLD SLASHER:
　　　　　Take this sword and die, sir!

ST GEORGE:
　I, sir?

BOLD SLASHER:
　　　　　Aye, sir!

ST GEORGE:
　　　　　Take your sword and try, sir!

[*They square up.*]

PROLOGUE:
　Here are two champions come to fight, that never fought before,
　But they will do the best they can—the best can do no more.

[*They fight.*]

　Fight on, fight on, my gallant boys, fight on, fight on with speed;
　Fight on, fight on, St George I'll vow, will kill Bold Slasher dead.

[*Slasher falls. Prologue turns to face St George.*]

　Bold Slasher now is dead, sir, and on the ground is laid,
　You'll have to suffer for it, I'm very sore afraid.

ST GEORGE:
>It was not I who did the deed—I don't know how he died.

PROLOGUE:
>How can you thus deny the deed, as I stood looking on?
>You drew your sword from out its sheath, and cut Bold Slasher down.

ST GEORGE:
>Oh dear, oh dear, what have I done?
>I've killed my father's only son!
>Around the company, round the hall,
>A five-pound doctor I must call.
>Is there a doctor in the house?

DR BROWN:
>In comes I, old Dr Brown,
>The best old doctor in the town.

ST GEORGE:
>How came you to be the best old doctor?

DR BROWN:
>By my travels.

ST GEORGE:
>Where have you travelled?

DR BROWN:
>England, Scotland, France and Spain,
>And here, to cure this man you've slain.

ST GEORGE:
>What can you cure?

DR BROWN:
>>I cure the dead.

ST GEORGE:
>The dead, you said?

DR BROWN:
>>I said the dead.

ST GEORGE:
>Stop, doctor, and try your skill.
>Cure this man—I think he's ill.

DR BROWN:
>What this same man that you did kill?

ST GEORGE:
>The very same.

DR BROWN:
>>Then take this pill.
>Now, all stand back and keep very still.

[*The pill takes effect, as is witnessed by convulsions and gurglings, till Bold Slasher leaps suddenly up and sings.*]

BOLD SLASHER [*sings*]:
    Once I was dead, but now I'm alive—
    God bless the doctor that made me revive!
    O brother, O brother, why drew you sword to me?
    But since I'm alive again, we'll shake hands and agree.

ST GEORGE [*sings*]:
    My brother's come alive again. We'll never fight no more—

ST GEORGE & BOLD SLASHER [*sing*]:
    We'll be as kind as brothers as we ever were before.

[*In Christmas performances, St George and Bold Slasher end their song with the additional lines,*
    With a pocketful of money and a cellar full of beer,
    We wish you a Merry Christmas and a Happy New Year!
*All then bow, before singing.*]

ALL [*sing*]:
    Now our play is ended and we can no longer stay,
    But with your kind permission, we'll be here another day,
    And before we go we'll have you to know, we'll have you to understand,
    Here's a health to St George, and success unto Merry England!

# MUSIC FOR THE PLAYS

# A-mumming we will go

Traditional

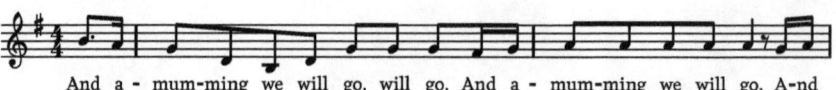

# Now our play is ended

Traditional

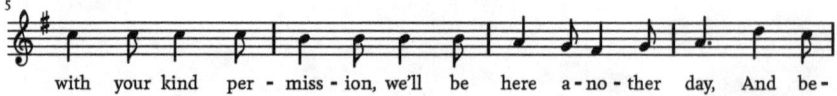

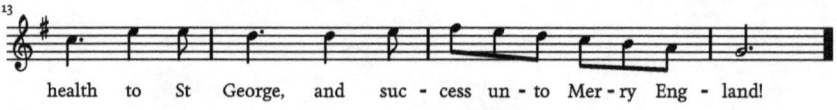

# Once I was dead

Traditional

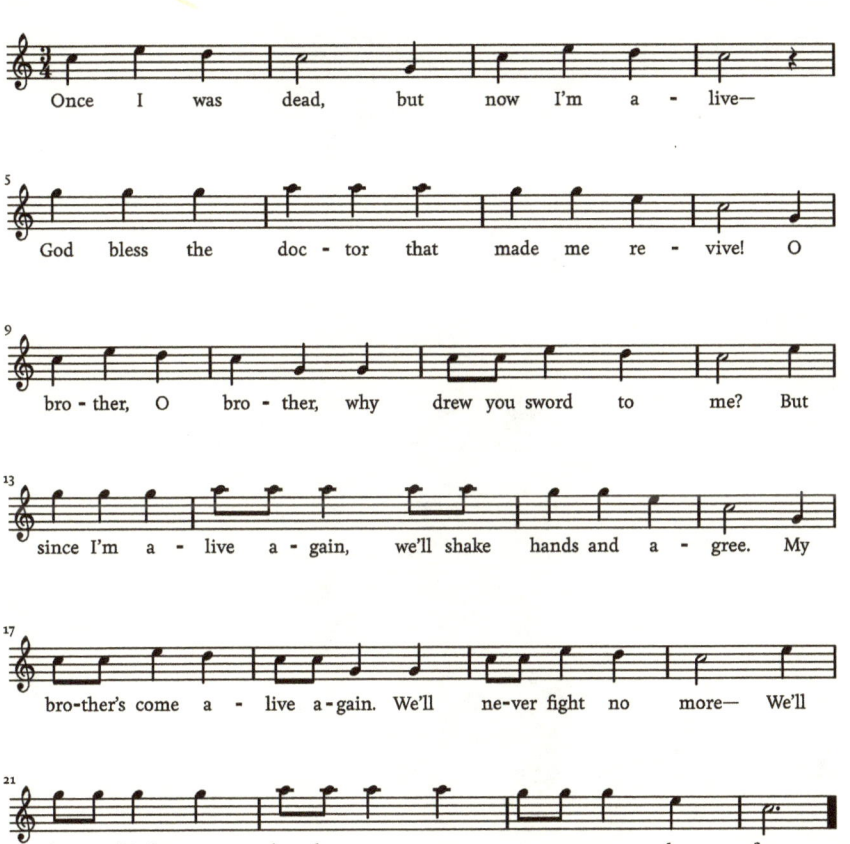

www.ingramcontent.com/pod-product-compliance
Lightning Source LLC
Chambersburg PA
CBHW031422040426
42444CB00005B/678

9 781910 075104